FLOWER GARDEN

WRITTEN BY

Eve Bunting

ILLUSTRATED BY

Kathryn Hewitt

Harcourt
SCHOOL PUBLISHERS

Orlando   Austin   New York   San Diego   Toronto   London

Visit *The Learning Site!*
www.harcourtschool.com

Printed in the United States of America

ISBN 0-15-341029-9

1 2 3 4 5 6 7 8 9 10   071   10 09 08 07 06 05 04

Garden in a shopping cart
Doesn't it look great?

Garden on the checkout stand
I can hardly wait.

Garden in a cardboard box
Walking to the bus

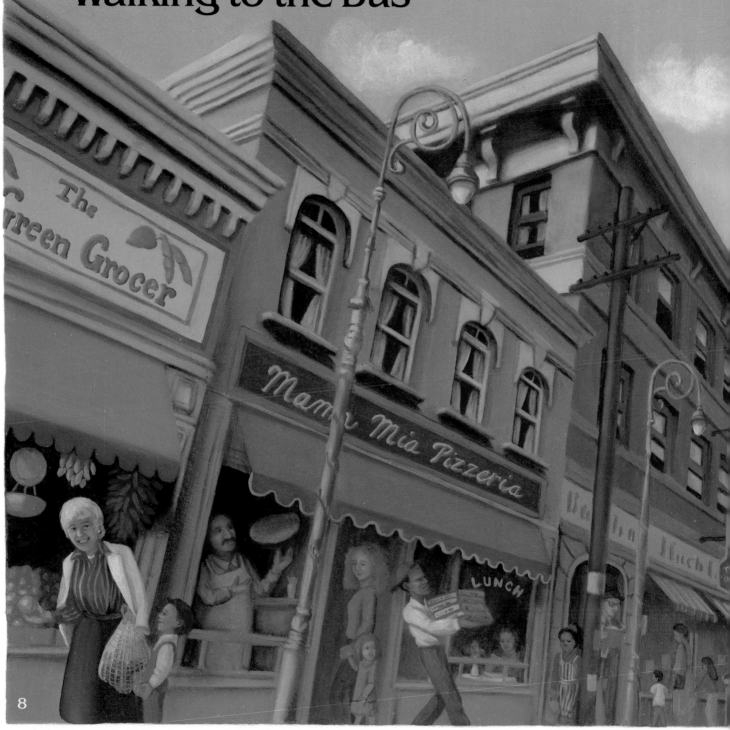

Garden sitting on our laps
People smile at us!

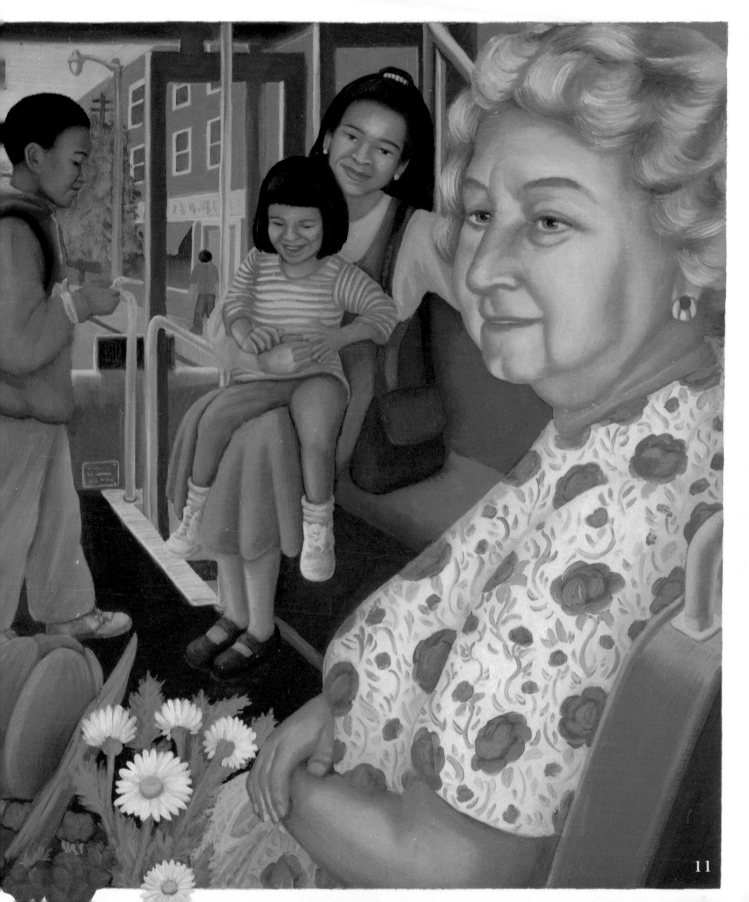

Garden going up the stairs
Stopping at each floor

13

This garden's getting heavier!
At last—our own front door.

Hurry! Hurry! Get the trowel
Spread the papers thick.

Get the bag of potting soil
Get the planting mix.

Put purple pansies at each end

Daisies, white as snow

Daffodils, geraniums and tulips in a row.

Garden in a window box
High above the street

Where butterflies
can stop and rest
And ladybugs can meet.

Walkers walking down below
Will lift their heads and see
Purple, yellow, red, and white
A color jamboree.

Candles on a birthday cake
Chocolate ice cream, too.

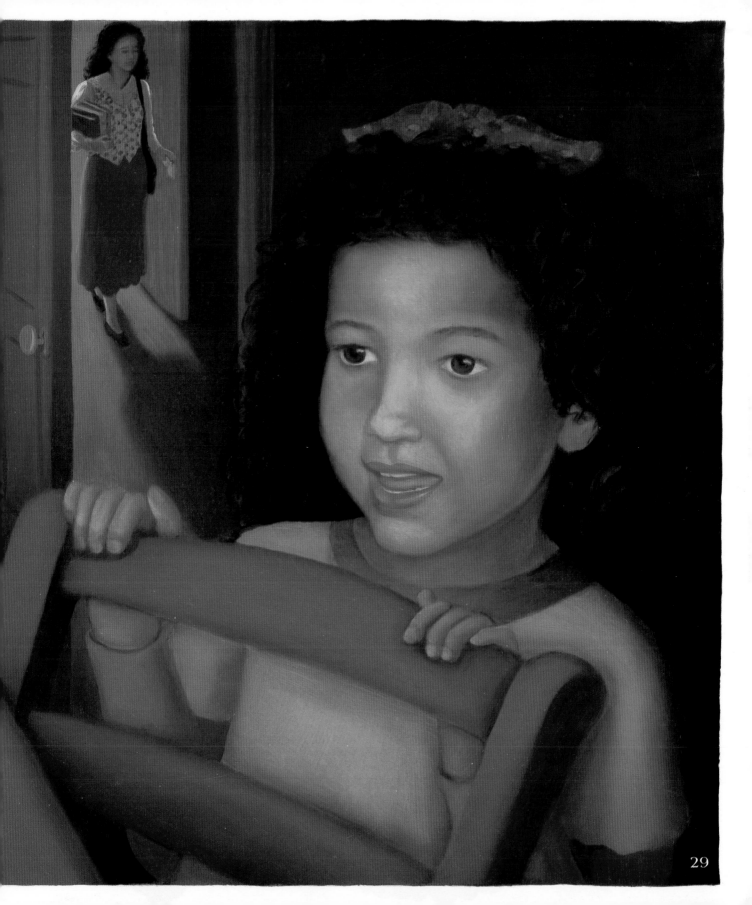

Happy, happy birthday, Mom!
A garden box — for you.

ISBN 0-15-341029-9

90000 >

9 780153 410291

Harcourt